# Scruffy at the Show

by Ian MacDonald

illustrated by Alex Paterson

This is Scruffy. Scruffy is an alpaca. He is Jen's pet and best pal!

They are off to the summer show. Jen is confident Scruffy will win 'Best Pet'.

Jen scrubs Scruffy in the bath.

She brushes him with a hairbrush.

She rubs each
hoof clean.

She ties a bow
in his hair.

Jen is proud of Scruffy.

They set off down the road. Jen keeps Scruffy on a tight lead.

At the farm, a donkey is eating hay. Scruffy likes hay, so he trots across.

The hay tickles the donkey's nose. It makes him snort. Hay flies in the air!

Cars, buses and trucks zip past. The dust spins and swirls.

Next, a man is cutting his lawn. The cuttings spray up.

In the park, children are playing football.
Scruffy likes children.

The children pat Scruffy. Soon, Scruffy is dirty with handprints.

"Oh dear!" cries Jen.

Scruffy and Jen walk under leafy trees.
Scruffy's bow gets tangled on a twig!

At last, they reach the show. Stands are laid with cakes and buns. Bunting flaps in the soft wind.

A girl spins candyfloss in a tub. Jen pulls on Scruffy's lead.

Too late!

Children smile and chuckle.

"Look! An alpaca with a pink beard," the children say.

Jen tugs Scruffy away.

“Quick, let’s get to the Best Pet ring,” says Jen.

A crowd forms as the pets arrive.

"They all look so smart!" Jen exclaims.

Two hounds, a hamster and a sleepy goat all stand in line.

“Not you!” says the man in a hat.
“What a state you are!”

Jen turns to go home.

“Come on, Scruffy,” she says sadly.

Then somebody shouts.

"Wait! You win the prize for ...

... Best Pet who looks like their owner!"

# Alpacas

Farmers keep alpacas for their wool. Alpacas can make good pets, too.

Encourage students to describe Scruffy as well as they can.